Something to Sing About
ACCORDING TO
Oscar Brand

For our children, our grandchildren, and other creations of which we are proud.
— The Brands

CONTENTS

3 Something to Sing About (Canadian version)

5 Something to Sing About (American version)

6 A Guy Is a Guy

8 When I First Came to This Land

SHOWS AND AMERICAN HISTORY

10 When Will I Learn (from "The Education of H*Y*M*A*N K*A*P*L*A*N")

12 All American (from "The Education of H*Y*M*A*N K*A*P*L*A*N")

14 Loving You (from "The Education of H*Y*M*A*N K*A*P*L*A*N)

16 Love Will Come (from "The Education of H*Y*M*A*N K*A*P*L*A*N")

19 Joyful Noise (from "A Joyful Noise")

23 Longtime Traveling (from "A Joyful Noise")

27 When You Meet Her (from "Thunder Bay")

28 My Two Hands (from "Thunder Bay")

30 I'm Afraid to Go Alone (from "Thunder Bay")

31 Comes the Right Man (from "How to Steal an Election")

32 Down Among the Grass Roots (from "How to Steal an Election")

34 Charisma (from "How to Steal an Election")

35 Mr. Might've Been (from "How to Steal an Election")

37 Sing America Sing

38 Song of the Presidents

40 Revolutionary Alphabet

THE AMERICAN DREAMER

41 Touch the Earth

42 First He Told Me

44 Remember the Horse

46 A Very Nice Country

48 There Were No Yellow Ribbons for Us

50 The Leaves Turn to Paper

COMMENTARY, MOSTLY HUMOROUS

51 Itazuke Tower

52 Appendectomy-Country Style

53 Cat Rap

54 Good Old Dog

56 What'll We Do With the Baby-O

58 Stretch Pants Lament

59 Skier's Daydream

60 My Old Man's a Sailor

62 Roll Your Leg Over

63 Violins Play Along

THE CHRISTMAS SEASON

64 Mary Had a Cousin

65 Who Knows the Color of God

66 Wake Up, Brother John

68 Burgundian Carol

69 Here It Comes

70 A Really Remarkable Star

72 Turn To Me

ISBN 978-1-4803-6658-9

Hollis Music, Inc.

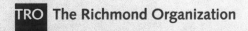 The Richmond Organization

EXCLUSIVELY DISTRIBUTED BY

HAL•LEONARD®
CORPORATION
7777 W. BLUEMOUND RD. P.O. BOX 13819 MILWAUKEE, WI 53213

www.oscarbrand.com

Oscar Brand

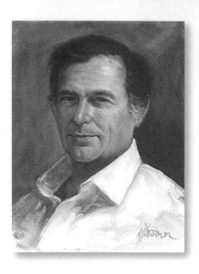

Singer/songwriter Oscar Brand was born February 7, 1920 in Winnipeg, Manitoba, Canada. He moved to New York as a young man, graduated from Brooklyn College and immersed himself in the burgeoning folk music scene where he met (and played alongside) such legends as Lead Belly, Woody Guthrie, Paul Robeson, Josh White Sr., Pete Seeger, Jean Ritchie, Theo Bikel, and Alan Lomax.

Simultaneously with his songwriting and performing career, in 1945 Brand began hosting the WNYC public radio show *Oscar Brand's Folksong Festival*, which included appearances by Lead Belly, Woody Guthrie, Pete Seeger, Theo Bikel, Harry Belafonte, the Kingston Trio, Peter, Paul & Mary, Dave Van Ronk, Judy Collins, Bob Dylan, Joan Baez, Phil Ochs, Harry Chapin, Arlo Guthrie, Emmylou Harris and many others. The show continues to be broadcast weekly, with an assist from Jean Ritchie's son, Jon Pickow, and has become the longest running program in the history of American radio. In the early 1960s Brand also broadcast his CTV television program *Let's Sing Out* from university campuses across Canada featuring Canadian artists, Joni Mitchell and Gordon Lightfoot among others.

By 1952 he had a No. 1 hit with Doris Day's recording of "A Guy Is A Guy" and "Burgundian Carol" was recorded by The Weavers. "When I First Came to This Land" became popular among folksingers and the text has appeared as a children's book His Canadian anthem "Something to Sing About" has become well known throughout Canada from the early 60s to this day. Recently he was honored with the Order of the Buffalo Hunt Award by the province of Manitoba.

Brand's score for the popular 1968 Off-Broadway show *How To Steal An Election* sent up the current belief that charisma would help a candidate win. In the late 60s Brand co-wrote two Broadway shows with Paul Nassau, *A Joyful Noise* and T*he Education of Hyman Kaplan*. Another Oscar Brand musical *Thunder Bay* based on Robert Ardrey's play Thunder Rock had a run in 1979 at the White Barn Theater in Connecticut.

The Kennedy Center 1976 bicentennial musical *Sing America Sing* was written and directed by Oscar who also performed in the show alongside John Raitt and other stars.

Other honors include serving on the board that created the Children's Television Workshop, the genesis of *Sesame Street*. The character Oscar the Grouch is based on Mr. Brand who had some policy issues. In 1982, he won the Peabody Award for broadcast excellence for the NBC *Sunday Show* and shared the 1997 Personal Peabody Award with Oprah Winfrey. Founding director and long time board member of The National Academy of Popular Music and Songwriters' Hall of Fame, he has received its Board of Directors highest award for distinguished service.

Oscar Brand is known for his wit as writer and performing artist on over 90 recordings with such wide ranging subjects as sports cars, the medical profession, pets and bawdy songs and ballads. As author his scholarship is evident in *The Ballad Mongers, Songs of '76/A Folksinger's History of the Revolution* and *Singing Holidays*.

Brand remains active today at 93 writing and performing, producing radio programs and in his spare time, writing his autobiography, *One Helluva Ride*.

For more information about Oscar Brand including available recordings, please visit his website www.oscarbrand.com.

Something to Sing About

(Canadian version)

Words and Music by
OSCAR BRAND

Additional Lyrics

3. I have heard the wild wind sing the places that I have been,
   Bay Bull and Red Deer and Strait of Belle Isle.
   Names like Grand Mère and Silverthrone, Moosejaw and Marrowbone,
   Trails of the pioneer, named with a smile.
   (Chorus)

4. I have wandered my way to the wild wood of Hudson Bay,
   Treated my toes to Quebec's morning dew.
   Where the sweet summer breeze kissed the leaves of the maple trees,
   Sharing this song that I'm singing to you.
   (Chorus)

5. Yes, there's something to sing about
   Tune up a string about
   Call out in chorus or quietly hum
   Of a land that's still young
   With a ballad that's still unsung
   Telling the promise of great things to come.
   (Chorus)

Something to Sing About

(American lyic version)

Words and Music by
OSCAR BRAND

I have wandered my way through the wonders of New York Bay,
North to Niag'ra to hear the falls roar,
Seen the waves tear in vain at the rock-covered coast of Maine,
Watched them roll back from the New England shore.

CHORUS
From the fair Hawaiian Islands to the Rocky Mountain Highlands,
'Cross the prairies, the plains to the mighty eastern towers,
From Alaska to the great Southwest, north to New England's crest,
Something to sing about, this land of ours.

I have heard the wild winds sing of places where I have been,
Backbone and Temperance, Whiskey and Sin,
Names like Wild Rice and Badger Jaws, Set Down and Santa Claus,
Trails of the pioneers named with a grin. (Chorus)

I have welcomed the dawn to the highland of Oregon,
Seen the moon light up the soft southern dew,
Where the sweet morning breeze kissed the leaves of the citrus trees,
Whispering the song that I'm sharing with you. (Chorus)

Yes, there's plenty to sing about, tune up a string about,
 Glories we've known and the promise to be,
And when there's something we think is wrong, we don't just string along,
We raise our voices in disharmony. (Chorus)

A Guy is a Guy

Words and Music by
OSCAR BRAND

When I First Came to This Land

Words and Music by
OSCAR BRAND

1. When I first came to this land, I was not a wealth-y man. Then I built my-self a shack, I did what I could.
2. When I first came to this land, I was not a wealth-y man. Then I bought my-self a cow, I did what I could.
3. When I first came to this land, I was not a wealth-y man. Then I bought my-self a horse, I did what I could.
4. When I first came to this land, I was not a wealth-y man. Then I bought my-self a duck, I did what I could.

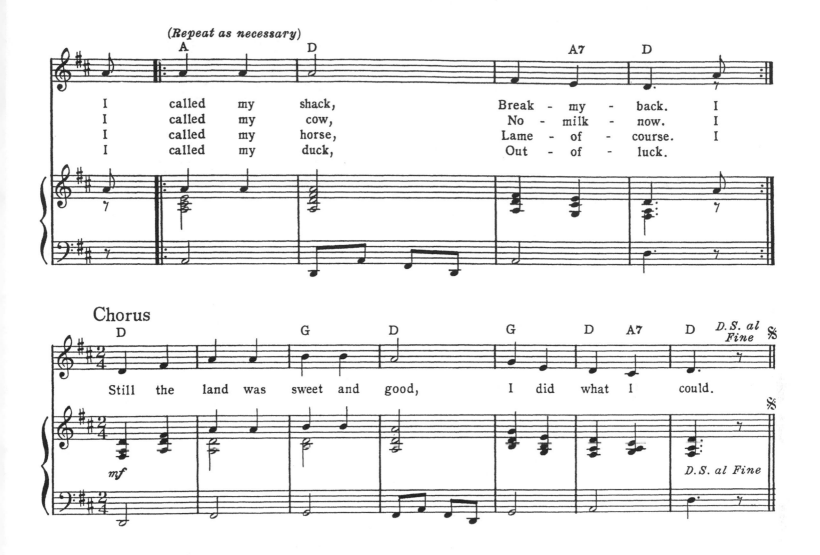

5. When I first came to this land, I was not a wealthy man.
   Then I got myself a wife. I did what I could.
   I called my wife, Joy - of - my - life,
   I called my duck, Out - of - luck,
   I called my horse, Lame - of - course,
   I called my cow, No - milk - now,
   I called my shack, Break - my - back.

   CHORUS

6. When I first came to this land, I was not a wealthy man.
   Then I got myself a son, I did what I could.
   I told my son: "My work's done".

   CHORUS: For the land was sweet and good,
                I did what I could.

From the Broadway musical production "The Education of H*Y*M*A*N K*A*P*L*A*N"

When Will I Learn!

Words and Music by
PAUL NASSAU and OSCAR BRAND

From the Broadway musical production "The Education of H*Y*M*A*N K*A*P*L*A*N"

All American

Words and Music by
PAUL NASSAU and OSCAR BRAND

1. Look at us walk-in' down the street, oh what a love-ly bunch, Com-i-cal crew, Peo-ple that you
2. May-be we're wear-ing coun-try clothes, May-be we're talk-ing wrong, May-be our style's, good for a smile,

would-n't in-vite for lunch, What a pa-rade of fun-ny folk, hap-pi-ly un-re-fined
may-be we don't be-long, Yet in this new and diff-'rent world, one thing is ver-y clear

Peo-ple may stare, what do we care, some-thing is on our mind.
Start-ing to-day, we're on our way, fun-ny or not we're here.

From the Broadway musical production "The Education of H*Y*M*A*N K*A*P*L*A*N"

Loving You

Words and Music by
PAUL NASSAU and OSCAR BRAND

Loving You-2

From the Broadway musical production "The Education of H*Y*M*A*N K*A*P*L*A*N"

Love Will Come

Words and Music by
PAUL NASSAU and OSCAR BRAND

Medium, with a definite beat

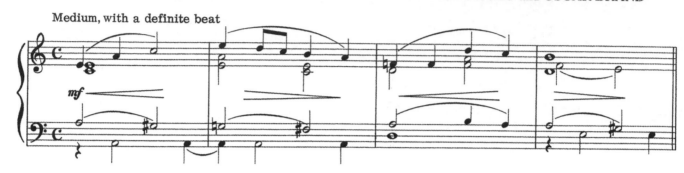

Love Will Come, how could I doubt it? Love Will Come, af - ter a while,
* Love Will Come, time will ar-range it, Love Will Come, where now is none,

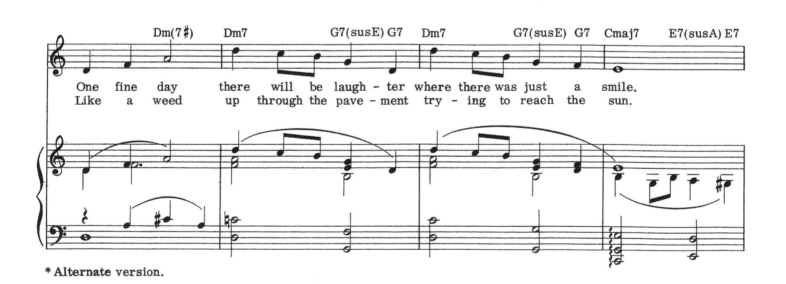

One fine day there will be laugh - ter where there was just a smile.
Like a weed up through the pave - ment try - ing to reach the sun.

* Alternate version.

A Joyful Noise

Words and Music by
PAUL NASSAU and OSCAR BRAND

From the Broadway musical production "A Joyful Noise"

Longtime Traveling

Words and Music by
PAUL NASSAU and OSCAR BRAND

Medium tempo

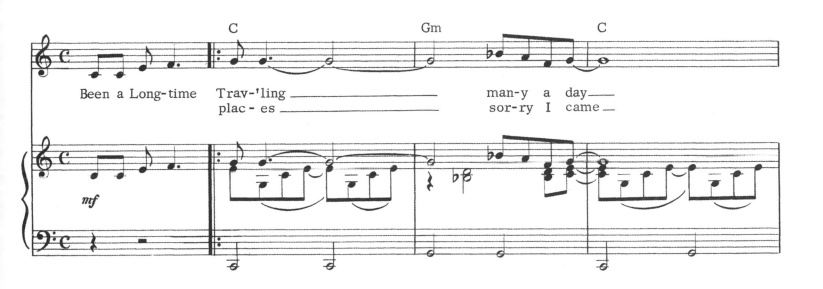

Been a Long-time Trav-'ling _____ man-y a day___
plac - es _____ sor-ry I came___

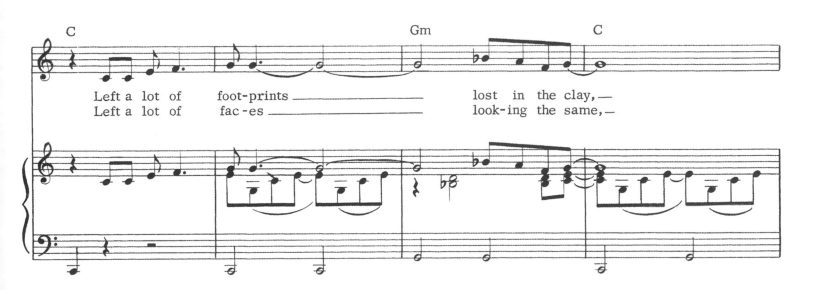

Left a lot of foot-prints _____ lost in the clay,—
Left a lot of fac-es _____ look-ing the same,—

From the musical production "Thunder Bay"

When You Meet Her

Words and Music by
OSCAR BRAND

Moderately

When you meet her____ will you tell her____ I en-vy her mo-ments with you?____ Her eyes that will

see you,____ her lips that will kiss you, Her fin-gers that will touch you as mine nev-er do.____ I must

leave you,____ but re-mem-ber;____ I loved you in my own fool-ish way.____ And I

en-vy her ev-'ry mo-ment with you, the girl you'll dis-cov-er some day.____ I have

no right____ to be jeal-ous,____ our love was a fu-tile de-sign,____ but I en-vy her ev-'ry

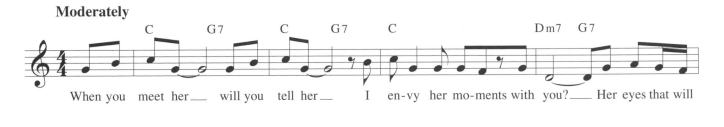

mo-ment with you, ev-'ry mo-ment that can nev-er be mine.____

From the musical production "Thunder Bay"

My Two Hands

Words and Music by
OSCAR BRAND

From the musical production "Thunder Bay"

I'm Afraid to Go Alone

Words and Music by
OSCAR BRAND

Moderate waltz

I'm a-fraid to go a-lone, in-to a world I've nev-er known, A shad-ow world that's
strang-er in the crowd, late-ly come but half al-lowed, Sud-den-ly a-

nev-er known of me. I'm a-fraid to walk a-lone in-to a mys-ter-y._____ To be the
mong, but not yet in. Wait-ing for the rit-u-al of wel-come to be-

-gin._____ I need some-one to go with me, some-one to know with me, The mes-sen-ger of

fear with-in the palm,_____ Who'll know the mo-men-tar-y death, in ev-'ry sud-den

spill of breath, Who'll hold me safe un-til the wind is calm._____ I need

some-one I can touch, some-one whose love for me is such, That I'm safe with-in the land-scape of my

past. Hold me fast,_____ be my sweet fa-mil-iar, And I'll suf-fer the un-known.

Come with me, come with me, I'm a-fraid___ to go a-lone.___

From the musical production "How to Steal an Election"

Comes the Right Man

(Ballad)

Words and Music by
OSCAR BRAND

From the musical production "How to Steal an Election"

Down Among the Grass Roots

Words and Music by
OSCAR BRAND

Additional Lyrics

2. Down among the grass roots where they put the fix in,
   Humphrey kills McCarthy, Rocky bows to Nixon,
   Where they manufacture all that large selection
   Of the lies they take back after the election,
   Down among the grass roots, that's where the fun begins.

   Down among the grass roots where the Red Alert is,
   Underneath the carpet, that's where all the dirt is,
   Where the simple folks insist on law and order
   Even if it takes a shotgun or a mortar,
   Down among the grass roots, that's where the fun begins.

   Down among the grass roots, picking through the daisies,
   Trying our best to sort the fringes from the crazies,
   Close to Mother Nature where the insects flourish,
   Meeting with the low lifes fertilizers nourish.
   Down among the grass roots where you must admit
   You don't shut your mouth, you'll get it full of grit.
   Down among the grass roots, that's where the fun begins.

From the musical production "How to Steal an Election"

Charisma

Words and Music by
OSCAR BRAND

Charisma

Habanera tempo

Am — D — G — A — G
Cha - ris-ma, cha - ris-ma, cha - ris-ma, cha - ris-ma, cha - ris-ma, cha-

A — D — Am — D — G
ris-ma, cha - cha - ris-ma!_____ Cha - ris-ma, cha - ris-ma, cha - ris-ma, cha-

A — G — A — 1. D — 2. D
ris-ma, cha - ris - ma, cha - ris-ma, cha - ris - i - ma!_____ ris - i - ma!_____

From the musical production "How to Steal an Election"

Mister Might've Been

Words and Music by
OSCAR BRAND

Moderate rock

C⌀ — Gm7/C — C
Mis - ter Might - 've Been, was it just a dream?_____ Were we fool - ish,
Were the words you spoke ev - er real - ly said?_____ Were they on - ly

Gb/C Gb/E — F — G/F Fm7
swim - ming a - gainst the stream?_____ Were we just chil - dren at play? Wast - ing our mo - ments a -
some - thing in - side my head?_____ I - de - as that had to be heard. Feel - ings that want - ed a

Bb/F C — Bb — 1. C Gm7/C — 2. C
way? Much too young to win, Mis - ter Might - 've Been._____ Been._____ Now the
word. Wait - ing to be - gin, Mis - ter Might - 've

From the 1976 Bicentennial Kennedy Center TV Production

Sing America Sing

Words and Music by
OSCAR BRAND

Bright March

You know the high road to free-dom is a hard road to trav-el. It's
start-ed our song when the truth was self ev-i-dent,

nev-er been eas-y to make free-dom ring. But when it's
choos-ing our lib-er-ty 'stead of a king. And what

not go-ing right by the dawn's ear-ly light Sing A -
ev-er comes in-to view, what do we al-ways do? Sing A -

mer-i-ca, Sing. We Sing. We took
mer-i-ca,

plen-ty of de-tours to trou-ble and glo-ry. Plen-ty of

side roads re-port-ed in song... But what ev-er we're go-ing through,

what do we al-ways do? Sing A-mer-i-ca, Sing.

From the Oscar Brand recording "Presidential Campaign Songs"

Song of the Presidents

Words and New Music Adaptation by
OSCAR BRAND

Medium Folk

1. George Wash-ing-ton was first in war and first a-mong our pres-i-dents, Next,
2.- 12., *See additional lyrics*

Ad-ams, his Vice Pres-i-dent, as lead-er took up res-i-dence. The

peo-ple turned to Jef-fer-son be-cause their cause he plead-ed, James

Mad-i-son___ and the Brit-ish war___ of eight-een twelve suc-ceed-ed.

Additional Lyrics

2. Next, James Monroe who did bestow an era of good feeling,
   And John Q. Adams followed him, for extra power appealing.
   When Jackson won at New Orleans, the voters said, "We need him."
   Then he arranged for little Matt Van Buren to succeed him.

3. Tippecanoe stayed one short month, old William Henry Harrison,
   John Tyler finished up his term, but there was no comparison.
   Next, Mexico was challenged by James Polk, who took in Texas.
   Then Zachary Taylor ran and won, but slavery did vex us.

4. When Taylor died, Mill Fillmore tried, but never took his place, sir.
   And Franklin Pierce met troubles that he really couldn't face, sir.
   When bachelor Buchanan found he hadn't what was needed,
   They called on old Abe Lincoln and the southern states seceded.

   Cont'd....

Additional Lyrics

5. Lincoln won the Civil War, but then a bullet reached him.
   Andrew Johnson took his place, but Congress near impeached him.
   We next elected U.S. Grant, whose friends got busy stealing.
   Then Hayes, who wasn't bad, but won by wheeling and dealing.

6. Brave Garfield then presided well till Guiteau got too nervous.
   And honest Chester Arthur came with rules for civil service.
   New Jersey's Grover Cleveland tried to help the Indian nations.
   Ben Harrison brought six new states, but Indians got short rations.

7. Cleveland, then was twenty-fourth as well as twenty-second.
   And though McKinley humbled Spain, assassination beckoned.
   Teddy Roosevelt shook a stick at trusts who tried to bust us.
   William Howard Taft came next, and then became Chief Justice.

8. Though Woodrow Wilson fought a war, for peace he kept on toiling,
   And Harding died of shame because his Teapot Dome kept boiling.
   Then Coolidge, Silent Cal, took charge and never changed expression.
   Next, Herbert Hoover came to town and with him the Depression.

9. Roosevelt brought a brand New Deal, four terms in office winning.
   But Truman finished World War II, the Atom Age beginning.
   Ike Eisenhower took us from Korea without malice.
   The Peace Corps came with Kennedy, but he was shot in Dallas.

10. The war in Vietnam so troubled Johnson he retired.
    Then Nixon wooed the Chinese, but resigned lest he be fired.
    Next, Gerald Ford was sandwiched in, then Georgia's Jimmy Carter.
    But hostages and economics made his efforts harder.

11. Ronald Reagan took the lead and debt went through the ceiling.
    He went to meet the Soviets, for honest peace appealing.
    George Bush, the navy pilot, flew his plane in World War II,
    He learned of sea, and sand, of oil and mountain view.
    When he was done, he taught his son, the narrow road to powers.
    Then Clinton came to join the game, Obama filled the hours.

12. 200 years and more have passed since Washington's election.
    We haven't done too badly in the process of selection.
    The people choose their leader and then tell him where to lead 'em.
    And somehow we keep traveling on the road to peace and freedom.

From the book "Songs of '76/A Folksinger's History of the Revolution"

The Revolutionary Alphabet

Words and Music by
OSCAR BRAND

Moderately

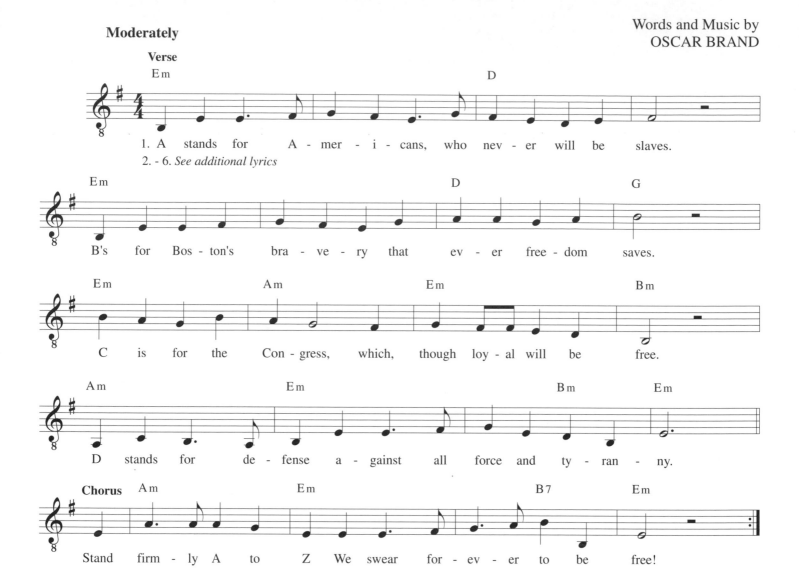

Verse

1. A stands for A - mer - i - cans, who nev - er will be slaves.
2. - 6. *See additional lyrics*

B's for Bos - ton's bra - ve - ry that ev - er free - dom saves.

C is for the Con - gress, which, though loy - al will be free.

D stands for de - fense a - gainst all force and ty - ran - ny.

Chorus

Stand firm - ly A to Z We swear for - ev - er to be free!

Additional Lyrics

2. E stands for the evils which a civil war must bring,
   F stands for a dreadful fate for people and for King,
   G's for George, may Heaven give him wisdom, health and grace,
   H is for the hypocrites who wear the double face.
   Chorus

3. J's for justice which the traitors now in pow'r defy,
   K's the King again, who should to such the axe apply,
   L's for London where he sits, to Honor ever true,
   M's for Mansfield, who, it seems, doth hold another view.
   Chorus

4. N is North who to the House the evil mandate brings,
   O's for oaths, which seemingly bind subjects not their kings,
   P stands for the people who their freedom would defend,
   Q stands for the question, when will England's troubles end?
   Chorus

5. R stands for the Rebels, not in Boston, but at home,
   S stands for the Stuarts, sent by Whigs abroad to roam,
   T stands for the Tories who may try to bring them back,
   V stands for the villains who have well deserved the rack.
   Chorus

6. W must stand for Wilkes, who us from warrants saved,
   Y for York the New, now half-corrupted, half-enslaved,
   Z we give to Zero, which refers to Tory minions,
   Who threaten us with fire and sword to bias our opinions.
   Chorus

From the Oscar Brand recording "American Dreamer"

Touch the Earth

Medium Bluegrass

Words and Music by
OSCAR BRAND

From the Oscar Brand recording "American Dreamer"

First He Told Me

Words and Music by
OSCAR BRAND

© Copyright 2013 Gypsy Hill Music, Great Neck, NY

From the Oscar Brand recording "American Dreamer"

Remember the Horse

Words and Music by
OSCAR BRAND

Fast Bluegrass

Bm ... A

1. I'm hit-ting eight - y 'cause the sign says fif-ty, eight-y's the clos-est I get. I got my
2. *See additional lyrics*

arm hang-ing out of the win-dow 'cause __ that makes the wind whis-tle like a jet. I got one fin-ger on the

steer-ing wheel __ just to keep her stead-y of clumps, __ I'm tear-ing out chunks of old six-ty six. Does

Rubato

an - y - one re-mem-ber the horse? Does an - y - one re-mem-ber the horse? When you

Moderately

could-n't see the air and the leaves were green, __ And the road dust rushed up nice and clean. __ And

may-be you got there a lit-tle late, But the folks did-n't mind __ if they had to wait. And if you dozed __ and the

Fast Bluegrass *(straight 8ths)*

reins went slack, the horse knew the way and he'd bring you back. 2. I'm
3. I'm

hit-ting eight - y 'cause the car be-hind me is blow-in' his horn, __ head-lights blind __ me. I'm

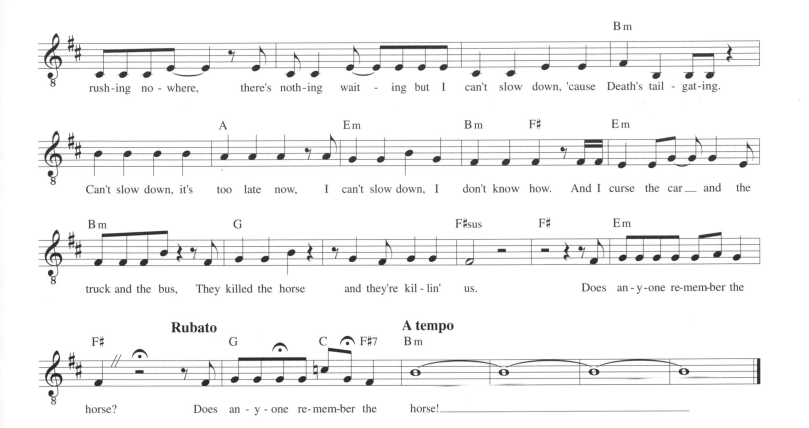

Additional Lyrics

2. I'm hittin' 80 'cause the truck can do it
No use wastin' the time
I got my eyeballs fixed like a rifle's sight
On that double dirty yellow line.
My headlight's cuttin' the gloom ahead,
I'm moving like a natural force.
I've got my foot pressed down on the mat,
Does anyone remember the horse?
Does anyone remember the horse?

When you tipped your hat when a friend walked by,
You looked straight up, you could see the sky,
The street was a place you could sit all day
And the park was a place you could eat and play.
And the air didn't rot out your hat and coat,
The wind didn't rasp at your nose and throat.

From the Oscar Brand recording "American Dreamer"

A Very Nice Country

Words and Music by
OSCAR BRAND

Soft Rock

Verse

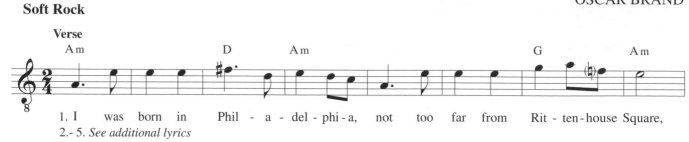

1. I was born in Phil - a - del - phi - a, not too far from Rit - ten - house Square,
2. - 5. *See additional lyrics*

May - be you pass by the place, some-time. My fam - i - ly still lives there.

But, please, don't ask them a - bout me... es - pe - cial - ly not my Dad,

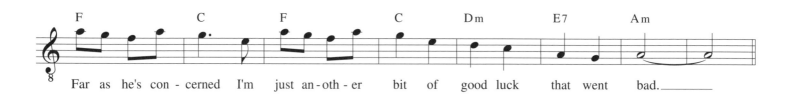

Far as he's con - cerned I'm just an - oth - er bit of good luck that went bad.____

Chorus

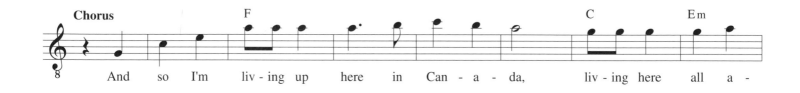

And so I'm liv - ing up here in Can - a - da, liv - ing here all a -

lone.____ A ver - y nice coun-try, but not my own.____

Additional Lyrics

2. Funny thing about the people here, they're just like the people back home
   And the buildings look a lot alike, not much of that New York chrome
   The streets are a little bit cleaner and every one has its sign,
   Printed very neatly, half a million streets, not one of them mine.
   Chorus

3. I keep writing lots of letters home. I get answers once in a while.
   Saying things like, "Please don't catch a cold." My Mom always makes me smile
   They never mention my brother or what he intends to be.
   Guess they're all afraid, if we got too friendly, he'll turn out like me.
   Chorus

4. Funny thing, the war is over now. They're not making anyone go,
   Seems as if they just got tired of it. And they used to love it so.
   You'd think they'd say, "We're sorry now, and maybe you were right,"
   But they won't let us back. They say it isn't fair to the kids they forced to fight.
   Chorus

5. There are lots of others living here, Twenty, thirty thousand or more,
   They say Lincoln granted amnesties, but that was another war,
   Besides, the government's much too busy now; it's foolish to make a fuss
   Trying to clear themselves of other crimes beside the one they pulled on us.
   Chorus

There Were No Yellow Ribbons For Us

Words and Music by
OSCAR BRAND

Moderately

1. I was just a high school drop-out, and it was-n't just a cop-out, I

2. - 4. *See additional lyrics*

thought I'd trav-el for a while,___ then go back home to mom.___ But my

trav-els were sus-pend-ed, I was draft-ed and up-end-ed, I

joined the might-y ar-my in the fields of Vi-et-nam. There were

tens of thou-sands fight-ing in the mud-dy fields___ of 'Nam, We

did our best___ with-out com-plaint or fuss. But when the war was

o-ver___ and we thought we'd be in clo-ver, There were no yel-low rib-bons___ for

us, There were no yel-low rib-bons for us.___

Additional Lyrics

2. My dad was one of millions in an army of civilians
   Who volunteered for service back in world war number II,
   And the way he tells the story,
   It wasn't games or glory
   But the country stood behind him, that's the one sure thing he knew.

   And the letters he received told him the folks were mighty proud,
   The town turned out when he got off the bus.
   We thought that we'd be heroes,
   But we ended up as zeros
   There were no yellow ribbons for us.

3. I remember one gray morning when the captain yelled a warning,
   But I guess I should forget it 'cause it wasn't very much.
   Just some shooting and some shelling,
   Some shouting and some yelling
   We had to drop our guns because they got too hot to touch.

   And our clothes were soaking wet from all the mud and blood and sweat,
   Our mouths were so damn dry we couldn't spit or even cuss,
   Well, I'm sorry that I started,
   But I get so damn downhearted.
   There were no yellow ribbons for us.

4. Sometimes I hear the crying of the wounded and the dying.
   I know I'll go down to my grave before the memory fades.
   That's all past but for the present,
   I didn't find it pleasant
   To see half a hundred athletes getting ticker tape parades.

   Sure I cheer them like the others, aren't all of them my brothers,
   Like the kids we left behind us - 57,000 plus.
   Now the memory's disappearing,
   But remember while you're cheering,
   There were no yellow ribbons for us.
   There were no yellow ribbons for us.

From the Oscar Brand recording "American Dreamer"

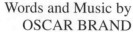

The Leaves Turn To Paper

Words and Music by
OSCAR BRAND

From the Oscar Brand recording "The Wild Blue Yonder"

Itazuke Tower

Words and Music by
OSCAR BRAND

Medium Bluegrass

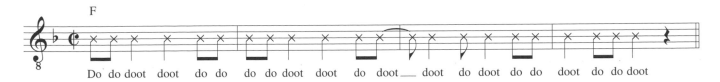

Do do doot doot do do do do doot doot do doot___ doot do doot do do doot do do doot

1. "It - a - zu - ke Tow - er, this is Air Force 8 0 1, I'm turn - ing on___ the down-wind leg, my
2. - 5., *See additional lyrics*

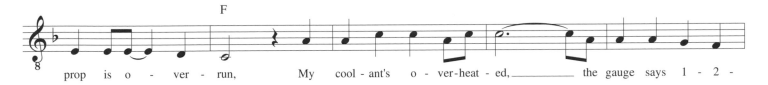

prop is o - ver - run, My cool - ant's o - ver-heat - ed,_____ the gauge says 1 - 2 -

1, You'd bet - ter get___ the crash___ crew out and get them on___ the run."

Additional lyrics

2. "Listen, Air Force 801, this is Itazuke Tower,
 I cannot call the crash crew out, this is their coffee hour,
 You're not cleared in the pattern now, that is plain to see,
 So take it once around again, you're not a V.I.P."

3. "Itazuke Tower, this is Air Force 801,
 I'm turning on my final, I'm running on one lung,
 I've gotta land this Mustang, no matter what you say,
 I'm gonna get my chart squared up before that Judgement Day."

4. "Now listen, Air Force 801, this is Itazuke Tower,
 We'd like to let you in right now but we haven't got the power,
 We'll send a note through channels and wait for the reply,
 Until we get permission back, just chase around the sky."

5. "Itazuke Tower, this is Air Force 801,
 I'm up in Pilot's Heaven, and my flying days are done,
 I'm sorry that I blew up, I couldn't make the grade,
 I guess I should have waited 'til the landing was OK."

From the Oscar Brand recording "For Doctors Only"

Appendectomy – Country Style

(The McBurney Square)

Words and Music by
OSCAR BRAND

Bright Square Dance

1. Wash your hands and get them dry, Keep them clean and keep them high,
2.- 6. *See additional lyrics*

When you're sure that you are a-ble, Prom-en-ade up to the ta-ble and

get that ap-pen-dix, Lay it bare, We're do-ing the Mc-Bur-ney Square.

Additional Lyrics

2. Now drape that patient neat and tight.
Bare the quadrant of the lower right
Do si do and careful all
While you make an incision in that wall.
Right hand under, if you dare
Doing the McBurney Square.

3. Swing that knife blade, with a toss.
Along the muscles, not across
With your fingers then induce
The peritoneum to work loose.
You mustn't rip and you mustn't tear
Doing the McBurney Square.

4. When the cavity's been breached,
The secum and appendix reached
Put a purse string suture on the base
And sprinkle gauze pads round the place.
Duck for oyster, I declare
Doing that McBurney Square.

5. With a peritoneal cuff inside,
Crush, ligate and then divide
Swing your partner, I'll swing mine,
Paint the stump with iodine.
Now force it back again with care
Doing that McBurney Square.

6. Tie the purse string very tight,
Suture the peritoneum right
Let those muscles settle in,
Then count the pads and close the skin.
Salute the patient, collect your fee
You've done the appendectomy.

Cat Rap

Words and Music by
OSCAR BRAND

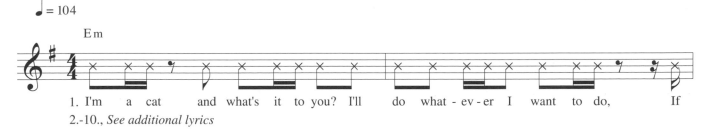

Em

1. I'm a cat and what's it to you? I'll do what-ev-er I want to do, If

2.-10., *See additional lyrics*

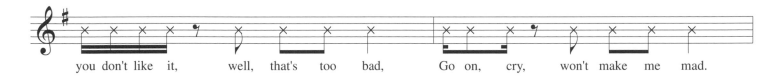

you don't like it, well, that's too bad, Go on, cry, won't make me mad.

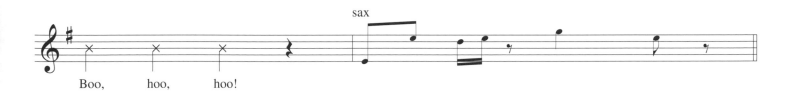

sax

Boo, hoo, hoo!

Additional Lyrics

2. But I'll tell you what burns me up,
   When you've just been patting some stranger's pup,
   Or another time you're out of line,
   When you come home with cat hairs and they're not mine.

3. And the litter ads that advertise,
   "Lasts for weeks," and you believe their lies,
   Sure, litter lasts two weeks or three,
   But that's more than I can say for me.

4. And there's another ugly scene,
   Just when I've licked myself all clean,
   You come home from some alien land,
   And rub me down with an unwashed hand.

5. And another thing gives me a pain,
   When you rub my fur against the grain,
   When you were just a human kitten,
   Didn't your mom teach you that that ain't fittin'.

6. Another thing that's rotten wrong,
   When you're out tom-catting all night long,
   And leave me lonely, no pats, no hugs,
   That's when I tear up the rugs.

7. And when you set out too much food,
   And I eat a lot but the rest gets glued,
   And you wonder why I don't eat the dregs,
   Well, baby, I hate ground horses legs.

8. My catgut needs fresh meat and fish,
   So don't put leftovers in my dish,
   Don't think I'm dumb enough to want it,
   Just 'cause you poured some gravy on it.

9. Well, them's a few of my complaints,
   I know that human beings ain't saints,
   But if you keep on bugging me,
   I'm going to throw up on your silk settee.

10. Just feed me, pet me, and we'll be great,
    Keep clean and I'll reciprocate,
    That's all there is, it's tit for tat,
    You treat me right, and I'm your cat.

From the Oscar Brand recording "Get A Dog"

Good Old Dog

Words and Music by
OSCAR BRAND

1. My Rob-in is a good old dog, The best there ev-er was.
Rob-in takes good care of me, The best I ev-er knew.
2. *See additional lyrics*

I love him 'cause he's smart and good; He loves me just be-cause. And
I love him though there's not much need; He loves e-nough for two. He

lays his paw u-pon my knee, In a way I can't ig-nore.

And if I scratch be-hind his ear, He loves me e-ven more. Bet he

knows what I've been say-ing, Ev-'ry sen-tence, Ev-'ry word. And I'll

bet his tail is wag-ging 'Cause he likes what he just heard.

Rob-in is a good old dog, And it should be no sur-prise.

He helps me see the world a-round, 'Cause Rob-in is my eyes.

Additional Lyrics

2. When I put the harness on him,
   And we go out for a walk,
   Robin knows just where to take me;
   I don't even have to talk.

   And I never have to worry,
   Just as long as he's in charge.
   And I know no one will harm me,
   'Cause he's really kind of large.

   When I feel him turning slightly,
   I know something's up ahead.
   Or a gentle pause informs me
   That the traffic light is red.

   We've walked many miles together,
   Since the time we first began,
   And I would trust him with my life,
   Just 'cause I know I can.

   Guess I couldn't do without him,
   And the wonder of it is
   Robin is a good old dog,
   I'm thankful that I'm his.

From the Oscar Brand recording "Sports Car/Songs for Big Wheels"

What'll We Do With the Baby-O?

Words and Music by
OSCAR BRAND

1. When I was a young man in my prime, I bought me an Olds-mo-bile on time; I
2.- 5., *See additional lyrics*

drove it hard and I drove it far __ and I loved the feel of a great big car. But I

mar-ried a gal __ who liked 'em small; She did-n't care for that Olds at all. I found the

ver-y best trade-in I could get; Spent my for-tune on a new Cor-vette. So,

What shall we do with the ba-by-o, What shall we do with the ba-by-o?

What shall we do with the ba-by-o, there's on-ly room for two.

Additional Lyrics

2. The first few years we were out all day watching nearby places fade away,
   Spent so much time on the open road, they'd have charged us rent if they only knowed.
   One day we were a-flyin' low, my wife says, "Honey, please take it slow."
   I thought my ears were a-playin' tricks and I saw her smile and the whole thing clicks.
   Chorus

Cont'd....

Additional Lyrics

3. Well, the baby come and it wasn't so bad, he sat in the front with his Mom and Dad.
   I bought him goggles and a driving cap, he looked right fine in his mother's lap.
   Sure he looked right fine 'till he up and grew, now the doggone kid obstructs my view.
   We shoulda known that he had to grow, but he's got too big and he's got to go.
   Chorus

4. So we put an ad in the Daily News, reading "One kid free complete with shoes."
   Answered all the calls and the letters but they'd end by saying, "You're off your nut."
   We left the kid in the woods one week, saying, "Cover your eyes, it's hide and seek."
   Drove away as fast as the car could tear; when we got home he was waiting there.
   Chorus

5. Well, we managed to jam in just one more by cutting a hole in the luggage door,
   So whenever we go out for a ride, he sits in the trunk with his head outside.
   Today I suffered another blow, my wife starts again with that "Take it slow."
   It looks this time like we're really sunk, there's no more room in the doggone trunk.
   Chorus:
   So, what shall we do with the baby-o, what shall we do with the baby-o?
   What shall we do with the baby-o, there's only room for three.

From the Oscar Brand recording "A Snow Job for Skiers"

Stretch Pants Lament

Words and New Music Arrangement by
RAY CONRAD
Additional Words by
OSCAR BRAND

Moderately

1. As I was out ski-ing___ one cold frost-y morn-ing,___ As
2.- 7., *See additional lyrics*

down the big moun-tain I gai-ly did go, I spied a young ski-er___ crashed

in-to the pine trees, Bur-ied___ neck deep in the cold, pow-der snow.

Additional Lyrics

2. "I can see by your outfit that you are a skier."
These words he did say as I christied about.
"Come linger beside me and hear my sad story,
I'm a young boomer who just got wiped out."

3. "It was once on my skis that I used to go swinging,
Once on my boards that I used to go fast,
Then I got me some stretch pants so I would look dapper;
Because of those stretch pants my ski days are past."

4. "Those stretch pants were handsome, those stretch pants
were lovely,
Those stretch pants were certain each skier to please,
But they had so much stretch, sir, that once I crouched down, sir,
I had not the strength, sir, to straighten my knees."

5. "Well, I wore them this morning to ski this here mountain,
I thought I would break these new pants in in style,
But the pants snapped me into a sitting position,
I lost my control and wound up in this pile."

6. "Oh, tell all my friends, sir that I went out bravely,
I went out like a man 'though I'm still in my teens,
Tell all my friends, sir, that though they'll look crummy,
They're safer by far if they ski in blue jeans."

7. And with this grim warning, his spirit departed,
We bitterly wept when the ski patrol came,
But early next morning we were all out in stretch pants,
Fearful or not, we were playing the game.

From the Oscar Brand recording "A Snow Job for Skiers"

Skier's Daydream

Words by RAY CONRAD
Additional Words by OSCAR BRAND
Music as sung and collected by
JEAN RITCHIE

Moderately

1. In the fall of the year, when the sum-mer grows old,_____ When the
2.- 4., *See additional lyrics*

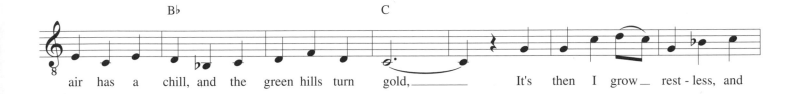

air has a chill, and the green hills turn gold,_____ It's then I grow_ rest-less, and

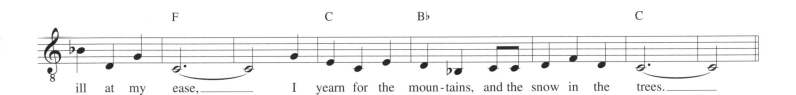

ill at my ease,_____ I yearn for the moun-tains, and the snow in the trees._____

Additional Lyrics

2. I think back on the glory of the days that have been
   And I know as I daydream there'll be good days again
   Or when the snows fly and the blizzard winds wail,
   I know that my ski tracks will show on some trail.

3. I'll go back to the mountains and the cold winter sun
   And the glitter of powder on a steep untracked run
   Where your breath shows as frost 'gainst the sky's brilliant blue
   And there's warmth and good friendship when day is through.

4. Oh, it may be some day when I've had my last run
   When I've hung up my skis, my life here is done,
   Well, if heaven's really heaven and that's where I go,
   There'll be frost on the mountain and deep powdered snow.

My Old Man's a Sailor

Words and Music by
OSCAR BRAND

Additional Lyrics

2. My old man's an anthropologist, what do you think of that?
   He wears an anthropologist's collar, he wears an anthropologist's hat.
   He wears an anthropologist's raincoat, he wears an anthropologist's shoes,
   And every Saturday evening, he reads the Sunday news.
   Chorus
   And someday, if I can,
   I'm gonna be an anthropologist, the same as my old man.

   Cont'd....

Additional Lyrics

3. My old man's a refrigerator repairman, what do you think of that?
   He wears a refrigerator repairman's collar, he wears a refrigerator repairman's hat.
   He wears a refrigerator repairman's raincoat, he wears a refrigerator repairman's shoes,
   And every Saturday evening, he reads the Sunday news.
   Chorus
   And someday, if I can,
   I'm gonna be a refrigerator repairman, the same as my old man.

4. My old man's a cotton-picking, finger-licking, chicken plucker, what do you think of that?
   He wears a cotton-picking, finger-licking, chicken plucker's collar, he wears a cotton-picking,
      finger-licking, chicken plucker's hat.
   He wears a cotton-picking, finger-licking, chicken plucker's raincoat, he wears a cotton-picking,
      finger-licking, chicken plucker's shoes,
   And every Saturday evening, he reads the Sunday news.
   Chorus
   And someday, if I can,
   I'm gonna be a cotton-picking, finger-licking, chicken plucker, the same as my old man.

5. So, my old man's an odor-decoder in the Provision Division of the Brazilian Pavilion, what do you think of that?
   He wears an odor-decoder in the Provision Division of the Brazilian Pavilion collar, he wears an odor-decoder
      in the Provision Division of the Brazilian Pavilion hat,
   He wears an odor-decoder in the Provision Division of the Brazilian Pavilion raincoat, he wears an odor-decoder
      in the Provision Division of the Brazilian Pavilion shoes,
   And every Saturday evening, he reads the Sunday news.
   Chorus
   And someday, if I can,
   I'm gonna be an odor-decoder in the Provision Division of the Brazilian Pavilion, the same as my old man.

From the Oscar Brand recording "Bawdy Songs and Back Room Ballads"

Roll Your Leg Over

Words and Music by
OSCAR BRAND

Moderate waltz tempo

1. If all them young ladies was little white rabbits,
2.- 11. *See additional lyrics*

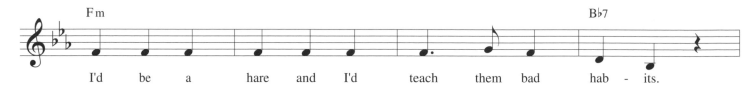

I'd be a hare and I'd teach them bad habits.

Chorus

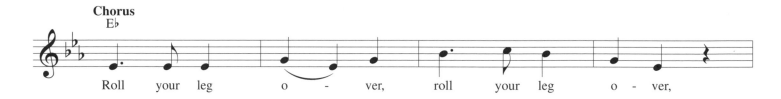

Roll your leg over, roll your leg over,

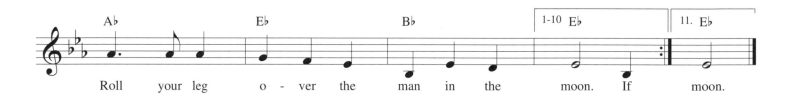

Roll your leg over the man in the moon. If moon.

Additional Lyrics

2. If all them young ladies was up for improvement,
   I'd give them some help with a ball-bearing movement. **Chorus**

3. If all them young ladies was little white kittens
   And I was the tom cat, I'd give them new fittin's. **Chorus**

4. If all them young ladies was B-29's,
   And I was a fighter, I'd buzz their behinds. **Chorus**

5. If all them young ladies was bats in a steeple
   And I were a bat---there'd be more bats than people. **Chorus**

6. If all them young ladies was diamonds and rubies
   And I were a jeweler, I'd shine up their boobies. **Chorus**

7. If all them young ladies was wheels on a car,
   Then I'd be the piston and go twice as far. **Chorus**

8. If all them young ladies was rushes a-growing,
   I'd take out my scythe and set out a-mowing. **Chorus**

9. If all them young ladies was bells in a tower,
   Then I'd be the sexton and I'd bang every hour. **Chorus**

10. If all them young ladies was bricks on a pile,
    Then I'd be the mason and I'd lay them in style. **Chorus**

11. If all them young ladies was singing this song,
    It would be twice as spicy and four times as long. **Chorus**

The Violins Play Along

Words and Music by
OSCAR BRAND

A and B sung simultaneously

A - B and C sung simultaneously

A - B - C and D sung simultaneously

A - B - C - D and E sung simultaneously (ending with ritard)

**From the Oscar Brand with The St. Pancras Boys' Choir recording
"Singing is Believing/Songs of the Advent Season"**

Mary Had a Cousin

Words and Music by
OSCAR BRAND

Additional Lyrics

2. The angel's name was Gabriel, a shining sight was he,
   And he also came to Mary in the land of Galilee.
   Saying, "The Lord has shown thy cousin and his power can be found
   And you shall have the Lord's own child before the year turns 'round.
   And your son shall be God's Holy One."
   Chorus

3. Since on Earth as up in Heaven, God's will is surely done
   Just as the angel promised her, the virgin had a son.
   And when the boys had grown to manhood, to the desert
   waste John strayed
   A-preaching of the Holy One for whom his people prayed.
   And behold Christ's reign as John foretold.
   Chorus

**From the Oscar Brand with The St. Pancras Boys' Choir recording
"Singing is Believing/Songs of the Advent Season"**

Who Knows the Color of God?

-ADVENT-

Words and Music by
OSCAR BRAND

From the Oscar Brand with The St. Pancras Boys' Choir recording
"Singing is Believing/Songs of the Advent Season"

Wake Up, Brother John

New Words and New Music Adaptation by
OSCAR BRAND

Brightly

Accompaniment - *sung as a traditional 2-bar round*

Frè - re Jac - ques, Frè - re Jac - ques, dor - mez vous? Dor - mez vous?

Son - nez les ma - tin - es! Son - nez les ma - tin - es! Din, dan, don. Din, dan, don.

Verses

1. Wake up, Broth - er John! Ring the bells for Christ - mas Day. Ring them loud,

bright and clear, ring in the best day of the year.

2. Wake up, Broth - er John! How can you sleep so late? The sign that should a - wak - en you, what

dream has o - ver - tak - en you? Ring in the best day of the year.

3. Wake up, Broth - er John! Soon it will be too late, With or with - out bells,

© Copyright 2013 Gypsy Hill Music, Great Neck, NY

Christ - mas won't wait. Noth - ing mat - ters in this Earth but the mem - 'ry of His birth.

That is the heart of it, please be a part of it. Ring in the best day of the year.

D
4. Wake up, Broth - er John! Too bad it's get - ting late, No bells shall ring - But wait! A

fly has crawled a - cross his nose. He turns, he snorts, he swats, he blows, he shakes, he

wakes! A sud - den cry: "It's Christ - mas Day!" Oh bless - ed fly. He's at the bel - fry,

starts to climb. Christ - mas bells will ring on time!_____

**From the Oscar Brand with The St. Pancras Boys' Choir recording
"Singing is Believing/Songs of the Advent Season"**

Burgundian Carol

French Carol
English Lyrics and Music Adaptation by
OSCAR BRAND

Evenly (♩ = 168)

Verse

1. The win-try sea-son of the year, When to this world our Lord was born, The
2.- 3., *See additional lyrics*

ox and don-key, so they say, did keep His Ho-ly Pres-ence warm.

Chorus

How man-y ox-en and don-keys you know, if they were there when

first___ He came, How man-y ox-en and don-keys you know at

such a time would do the same? As same?_____

Additional Lyrics

2. As soon as to these humble beasts
   Appeared our Lord, so mild and sweet,
   With joy they knelt before His grace,
   And gently kissed His tiny feet.
   Chorus

3. And on that night it has been told,
   These humble beasts so rough and rude,
   Throughout the night of holy birth,
   Drank no water, ate no food.
   Chorus:
   How many oxen and donkeys you know,
   Dressed in ermine, silk and such,
   How many oxen and donkeys you know
   At such a time would do as much?

From the Oscar Brand with The St. Pancras Boys' Choir recording
"Singing is Believing/Songs of the Advent Season"

Here It Comes

-NEW YEAR-

Words and Music by
OSCAR BRAND

Brightly

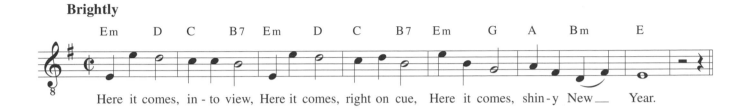

Here it comes, in - to view, Here it comes, right on cue, Here it comes, shin-y New ___ Year.

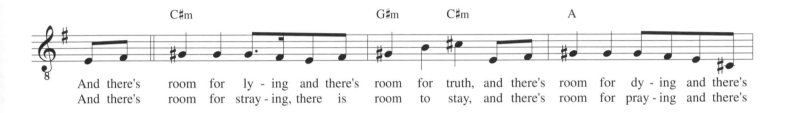

And there's room for ly - ing and there's room for truth, and there's room for dy - ing and there's
And there's room for stray - ing, there is room to stay, and there's room for pray - ing and there's

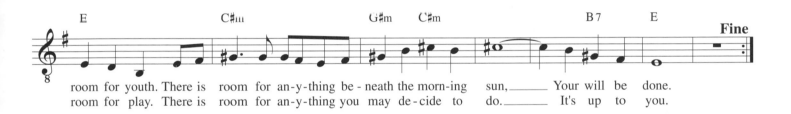

room for youth. There is room for an-y-thing be - neath the morn-ing sun, ___ Your will be done.
room for play. There is room for an-y-thing you may de-cide to do. ___ It's up to you.

Grab it all as you choose. It's a gift, Don't ask whose. You don't have to pay, you see, it's free.

From the Oscar Brand with The St. Pancras Boys' Choir recording
"Singing is Believing/Songs of the Advent Season"

The Really Remarkable Star

-EPIPHANY-

Words and Music by
OSCAR BRAND

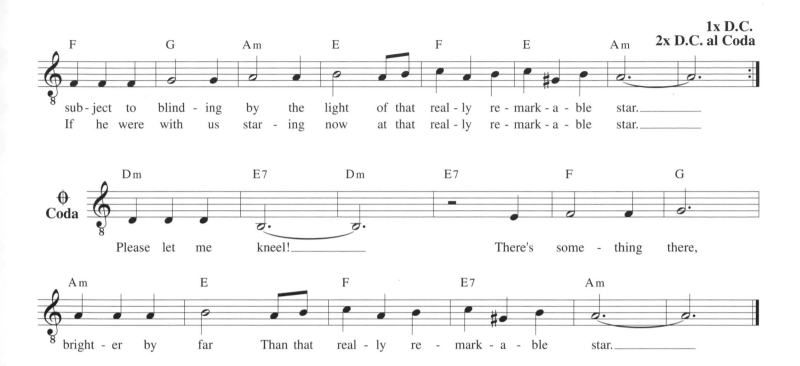

1x D.C.
2x D.C. al Coda

sub-ject to blind-ing by the light of that real-ly re-mark-a-ble star.____
If he were with us star-ing now at that real-ly re-mark-a-ble star.____

Coda

Please let me kneel!____ There's some-thing there,

bright-er by far Than that real-ly re-mark-a-ble star.____

From the Oscar Brand with The St. Pancras Boys' Choir recording
"Singing is Believing/Songs of the Advent Season"

Turn To Me

Words and Music by
OSCAR BRAND

Moderately

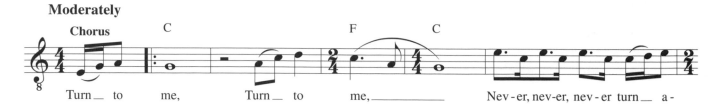

Turn__ to me, Turn__ to me,_____ Nev-er, nev-er, nev-er turn__ a-

way._____ I'll be wait - ing,__ I'll__ be wait - ing, wait and see,__ If you'll

turn,__ turn,__ turn__ to__ me.

1. When you're feel - ing down, I will raise you up,
2. When the world is wrong, I will make it right,

When you wear a frown, I will fill your cup. When your heart is sad, I will make you gay,
When the night is long, I will make it light. When you need a friend, I will un - der - stand,

When you're far from home, I'll show you the way._____ Turn to __ Turn__ to
When you've reached the end, I will take your hand._____